# Never Let Fear Dictate
# Your Life Ever Again

### *This Book Gives You 15 Ways to Bust Up Fear*
### *And Live a Bold Life That You Love*

So often our fear is unnecessary, and it is the biggest thing that stops us from moving forward.

In this thought-provoking book, Lucetta Zaytoun walks you through understanding your fears, letting them go, and bringing your goals and dreams to fruition.

There is no need for you to suffer and stay stuck any longer. You can push past your fears and design a life you actually love. It's possible!

Ask yourself:

- How much do I really love my life?
- What holds me back from fully living?
- Why do I let fear play such a big role?

Pick up a copy of this powerful book today and experience freedom in your life like never before!

*Michelle,*

*Make fear afraid of you!*

♡ *Lucetta*

# Your Amazing Itty Bitty® Fear-Busting Book

*15 Ways to Push Past Fear*

Lucetta Zaytoun

Published by Itty Bitty® Publishing
A subsidiary of S & P Productions, Inc.

Copyright © 2016 **Lucetta Zaytoun**

Printed in the United States of America

Itty Bitty® Publishing
311 Main Street, Suite D
El Segundo, CA 90245
(310) 640-8885


ISBN: 978-0-9992211-2-9

*This book is dedicated to you. May you come into your own magnificence by claiming your courage.*

*Courage is the fastest way to self-confidence.*
*~ Lucetta Zaytoun*

Stop by our Itty Bitty® website to find to interesting information about overcoming fear.

www.IttyBittyPublishing.com

Or visit **Lucetta Zaytoun** at

www.lucettazaytoun.com

# Table of Contents

Push 1.     Defining the Absurdity of Most Fear

Push 2.     Benefits of Pushing Past Fear

Push 3.     Examining the Basis of the Fear

Push 4.     Check Your Motivation

Push 5.     Stop Thinking You Are Not Enough

Push 6.     Bust Up Your Assumptions

Push 7.     Banish Self-Doubt. You'll Handle It

Push 8.     Make Fear Your Friend

Push 9.     Shrewdly Choose Your Support

Push 10.     Quit Using Fear as Your Security Blanket

Push 11.     Action Conquers Fear

Push 12.     Become the Badass You Are

Push 13.     Decide. The Rest is Details

Push 14.     Make YES Your Mantra

Push 15.     You've Totally Got This

# Introduction

You've got this, totally. Look back in your life and notice the times you've faced down fear, even in the many firsts of your youth. You learned to walk, ride a bike, went to your first day of school, graduated, had your first date, your first kiss, etc. These were uncomfortable, awkward, or scary at first, but look how you have grown from the experiences. Remember how exciting new things were when you were young?

The moment you get past your youth, you fall into patterns of being comfortable. You don't want to get out of your comfort zone or risk looking awkward or failing, so you become complacent and numb yourself by living your life in a rut. You think you are protecting yourself, yet often this means you are needlessly settling or suffering because you are afraid to change things.

Sometimes though, existence sends you a life smack and you are thrown out of your comfort zone beyond your control.

In this book, you will learn ways to push past your fears and live an exciting, adventurous life, whatever that looks like to you. So keep reading and embrace your courage and strength. You have so much more of it than you realize. The goal for this book is – at the end – rather than feeling fear, you will feel love for your courageous self. You can do this!

# Push 1
## Defining the Absurdity of Most Fear

Let's face it, 98% of fear is stupid. Anytime you are worried, anxious or fearful, it's in the future, which means it hasn't even happened yet. If it hasn't happened, it means you are making up a story. Let's figure this out.

1.  Fear lives in your head. As a human, you always go to worst-case scenarios. If you are making up a story, why not go to best-case scenario and live in that energy instead?
2.  The other 2% of fear is for your survival, when you are in a primal fight or flight situation. Nowadays in society, this rarely ever comes up in your life, yet you let needless fear dominate your thinking.
3.  Fear can also be an excuse to stay in your comfort zone.
4.  Understanding that most fear is completely unnecessary is amazingly freeing.

## What to Do When Crazy Fear Shows Up

- Step away and take three deep breaths. It actually lowers your blood pressure.
- Acknowledge the fear and notice the story you are making up.
- Rewrite that story into a positive. If you think it could go the worst way, why can't it go the best way?
- Take another deep breath.
- Claim the strong courage you have inside of you.
- Smile. Forming your lips into a smile can seriously change your mood.
- Take even one small step toward what you want, and watch the fear dissipate.
- Have faith in yourself. Faith that you are making the right decision for you.

*"You miss 100% of the shots you never take."*
*~ Wayne Gretzky*

# Push 2
## Benefits of Pushing Past Fear

It seems so much easier to just stay in the comfort zone, but actually that's exhausting as well. Often you are secretly suffering as you conform your life to the way it "should" be. Pushing past fear has many benefits for your body, mind and soul.

1. When you do something courageous, your self-confidence immediately goes up.
2. You become comfortable with being uncomfortable, which is amazingly freeing in your life.
3. You feel empowered and that ultimately makes you unstoppable in your quest.
4. You open yourself up to experiences that never would have happened.
5. You become inspiring to others, as they want to be as courageous as you.
6. This fearful experience could lead to something completely different that you could never have imagined.

## More Benefits of Pushing Past Fear

- Your shoulders go back and you stand tall.
- It helps with any future fears that may arise because you say to yourself, "If I did that, surely I can do this."
- You begin to love yourself for being so courageous.
- You buy into the thought that you make good decisions.
- Others see you as a total badass, which will delightfully shock you at first.
- You will eventually get to a point where basically nothing scares you.
- You will have the courage to let go of the things that no longer serve you.
- Loving life becomes your new normal.

*And the day came when the risk to remain in a tight bud was more painful than the risk it took to blossom.*

*~ Anais Nin*

# Push 3
## Examining the Basis of the Fear

Fear comes to you from many places and in many ways. Being able to pinpoint why and how it is showing up can make it easier to acknowledge it and let go.

1. As a human you will do anything to avoid pain. Your biggest fear is that you will be hurt physically, mentally or emotionally.
2. The truth is, as a human, pain happens to you anyway. And if you are going to feel pain, why not have it happen while going after something you want, rather than experiencing it because you are stuck or stagnant?
3. Was this fear given to you as a child from your parents' fears and it's not really even your own? Or did it come from a spouse, boss, ex lover, some relationship or past experience?
4. Is your fear coming from a lack of faith in yourself?
5. Acknowledge the origins of these fears and realize that they exist only in your past – they are gone, over. Start with now.

## More About The Basis of Fear

- Many people use fear as a security blanket and an excuse not to move forward in life.
- In that regard, fear is controlling you by dictating and limiting your actions.
- You are a grown adult and you deserve the freedom to live your life your way, doing what you love and being happy.
- It is more dangerous to give fear control because then it's difficult to achieve anything meaningful or significant in your life.
- The base of fear grows if you continue to give it time and attention. Stop the story in your head right away.
- For many, fear is based on disaster scenarios or worries about disappointing people. But what if that doesn't happen?

*Comfort zones are plush-lined coffins. When you stay in your plush-lined coffins, you die.*

*~ Stan Dale*

# Push 4
## Check Your Motivation

Often fear stems from not being clear about what you really want. Unsettled and indecisive is a very scary place to be. Let's check where your motivation comes from and see if you can grab some clarity, quelling those fears.

1.  Explore whether what you want is internally or externally motivated. So often you set yourself up by focusing on "I should" and "I need to" rather than "I want."
2.  Decision made from "should" and "need to" are externally motivated by others; society or culture. If this is where your desire comes from, then it is externally motivated, and with it comes a lot of fear because it's not really yours.
3.  Discover what you really want in life. When you get clear, you are internally motivated. Fear goes away and you become unstoppable because the power in you becomes amplified.
4.  This is your life. Live it in a way that works for you.

## More About Checking Your Motivation

- Take time to step away from your life and examine the motivation for your desires.
- Spend an afternoon in a park without your electronics and be with yourself. Think through your true yearnings.
- Ask yourself: Is my life where I want it to be?
- What's holding me back and what do I need to let go of to be truly happy?
- What have I really got to lose by changing things up and going after my dreams?
- A year from now, if I don't push past fear and make changes, what will my life look like?
- Can I continue to live with myself if I allow fear to stay in the driver's seat?

*You are the only person who wakes up every day and lives your life, so live it your way.*
                                   *~ Lucetta Zaytoun*

# Push 5
## Stop Thinking You Are Not Enough

Other people have done it and they don't have super powers. They are human just like you, so why can't you?

1. Feeling unworthy is like driving with the emergency brake on, and it will allow fear to slow everything down.
2. When someone exhibits courage they are still afraid while it is happening. They just do it scared. You can do the same.
3. What have you got to lose by going bold in your life? Not much actually, and you potentially have everything to gain. Pretty soon, you will feel like you are more than enough.
4. Why do you put other humans above you? Everyone has all the same fears and anxieties you have.
5. Claim all the frightening and courageous things you've already made it through.

## You are More Than Enough

- Be grateful for the life lessons you've learned which have brought you to this perfect place to push past your fears.
- Don't fear rejection because it's not about you, it's about them.
- If you are asking for something and get rejected, you haven't really lost anything; you didn't have that job or apartment or lover before. You can't lose what you don't already have, so ask.
- Truth be told, you are a badass. It has been smothered under your feelings of unworthiness. Let your inner strength come out of hiding. It is unbelievably empowering!
- What would you do if you felt 100% worthy?

*Worthiness doesn't have prerequisites.*
*~ Brene Brown*

# Push 6
## Bust Up Your Assumptions

You are an assumption-making machine. You make up hundreds of stories each day about everyone and everything! So much of your fear is based in assumptions. It's not reality; it's just all in your head. When you are fearful, ask yourself this question: "Am I making up a story about this?"

1. You think fear has been protecting you and helping you stay safe or avoid pain. That's an assumption. Unless you are in life-threatening danger, it is holding you back.
2. You make up stories: If I do this, they'll think that. They'll be mad, sad, hurt or lost. You don't actually know their response. It could be completely the opposite of what you made up.
3. You're human and sometimes humans disappoint each other, so hard times are going to have to be dealt with anyway. Why not deal with them while you are courageously going after your dreams?

## More About Busting Up Your Assumptions

- Ask yourself; "Are my fears based in fact or am I making up a story?"
- Say out loud, "I am NOT going to make up a worst-case scenario."
- "I'm going to push past fear and do what I need to do for me. I'll deal with the fallout later, and it might not even be as bad as I imagined."
- Start noticing all day long how you make up assumptions about everything and everyone.
- You make decisions on what you think you know. Bust through the setback that you believe your assumptions are real.
- Assumptions allow the best in life to pass you by.
- Check your assumptions at the door.


*Do the thing you fear and the death of fear is certain.*

*~ Ralph Waldo Emerson*

# Push 7
## Banish Self-Doubt. You'll Handle It

Every challenge potentially has the power to knock you on your knees, and your fear is that you won't withstand it.

1. You have incredible brainpower and lots of life experience under your belt. You'll figure it out.
2. You have a history of handling situations and making it through. Think about it.
3. If things do go awry, you'll figure out the next best step.
4. All you really need is a next best step. That step will inform the next, which will inform the next.
5. If it doesn't challenge you, it won't change you.
6. Are you allowing the fear of the after to dictate what you do now? You don't even know what the after is yet.

## More About Handling It

- You are alive and reading this book; that fact alone means you know how to make it through difficult situations.
- You gain strength, courage and self-confidence when you look fear in the face. Do it for you.
- Banish the fear of trying something new. Look at Thomas Edison and how he handled 10,000 screw-ups. He tried over and over again, refusing to give up.
- When you stay stuck, afraid of what will happen, you go nowhere. Then you are most likely suffering where you are.
- You are strong enough to face it all, even if it doesn't feel like it right now.

*Courage doesn't always roar. Sometimes courage is the quiet voice at the end of the day saying, "I will try again tomorrow."*
*~ Mary Ann Radmacher*

# Push 8
## Make Fear Your Friend

Fear and excitement physiologically manifest the same way in your body. The exact same thing happens if you are delightfully excited or shaking in your boots.

1.  What if you were to replace your inner voice of, "I'm afraid" with "I'm excited?"
2.  Sometimes being afraid is good because it means you care. If you didn't care, you wouldn't have this emotional response.
3.  Be scared, and care, and then do the scary thing anyway.
4.  If something scares you, that's a pretty good indicator that's exactly what you should be doing.
5.  Decide to embrace fear, knowing it will ultimately move you forward in your life.

## Making Friends With Fear

- Boldly claim out loud to Fear that you will triumph over it, and then give it a bro hug.
- Stars can't shine without the dark. Pushing past fear is what makes the joy of accomplishment so sweet.
- Fear is sometimes your greatest motivator.
- It's OK to be afraid. It means you are about to do something truly brave.
- There can be no courage unless you're scared. Embrace fear.

*Use your fear…it can take you to the place where you store your courage.*
*~ Amelia Earhart*

# Push 9
## Shrewdly Choose Your Support

When you are taking on changes in your life or going after a big dream, be careful with whom you share this journey.

1.  People can influence you positively or negatively and it's important to know the difference.
2.  Only share your plans with those people who truly have your back. The ones who make you feel your best when you are with them. They'll give you strength.
3.  Others may love you and don't mean to make you feel bad, but they do. This could even be a spouse, family member or a friend. Love them, but don't tell them yet.
4.  They will impose their feelings or fear about what you are doing in a negative way and take the wind out of your sail.
5.  Withhold your plans, or only give highlights to these people until you are fully launched and far enough into it that they can't dampen your spirit.

## More About Support

- Find your tribe of people who believe in you and share your dreams and plans with them.
- This could be anyone; a co-worker, a new acquaintance, or even the barista at your local coffee shop who thinks you're awesome.
- You will also be inspiring your people to go bold as well, so what if this wasn't just about you?
- During this time, surround yourself with people who make you feel like your best self. They will provide emotional, physical and intellectual support.

*Friends are medicine for a wounded heart, and vitamins for a hopeful soul.*

*~ Steve Maraboli*

# Push 10
## Quit Using Fear as Your Security Blanket

Humans are creatures of habit and resist things that would actually free us. Like other humans, you use fear as your excuse for not getting out of your comfort zone and moving forward. You hide behind fear.

1. Growth, expansion and development require some discomfort.
2. What if you were to take 100% responsibility for your actions and your life?
3. Don't make excuses such as blaming non-action on someone else. "Well I would do this, but my friend, spouse or family won't like it."
4. You may think that fear is protecting you, but unless your life is in danger, then it is actually hindering you.
5. You have more strength and courage than you realize. Throw that *blankie* in the trash.

## More About False Security

- 98% of your fears never come true. Would you miss this experience for that other 2%?
- So often you think it's easier to stay where you are, but if that's not working for you, then you are suffering.
- Would you rather suffer than take the chance of having a life you love and making your dreams come true?
- Remember that you always have a choice. You can choose to step up and claim that you will walk right past fear.
- Don't let fear dictate your life.


*Only those who will risk going too far can possibly find out how far one can go.*
*~.T.S. Elliot*

# Push 11
## Action Conquers Fear

A big part of your fear is in not knowing; not knowing what to do, where to turn, or what it will be like. Taking even a small action step can begin to give you clarity and information.

1. You don't have to have it all figured out. One step will inform the next which will inform the next.
2. Take the next best step. All you need at this moment is a next best step.
3. Find out more about the thing that gives you fear.
   a. Do research into how much apartments cost in that town.
   b. What that job description would include.
   c. How people make it as a single mom, etc.
4. The moment you dive in, even just a little, fear begins to dissipate because you get clearer.
5. Ask, ask, and ask. Ask for help, for information, for a hand, for a favor.

## More Action Conquers Fear

- All of your dreams can come true, if you have the courage to pursue them.
- A little progress each day adds up to big results.
- Be fearless in the pursuit of what sets your soul on fire.
- Courage is taking one more step than you think you can.
- Actions show where your priorities are.
- Your actions will tell you everything you need to know.

*The successful person makes a habit of doing what the failing person doesn't like to do.*
*~ Thomas Alva Edison*

# Push 12
## Become the Badass You Are

Do you look at other brave people and say, "I
wish I could do that" or "I wish I was like that."
You can do those things and be like that person.

1. Fear is the only thing standing in the way
   of you claiming your own magnificence.
2. You are stronger than you know, braver
   than you believe, and smarter than you
   think you are.
3. Be authentically you, not who you think
   you "should" be. These are the very
   things people love about you. There is
   nothing more badass than being yourself.
4. When you break out your badass, you
   become magnetic. People want to brush
   up against you and be inspired. They say,
   "I want what they have."

## More about Badassery

- Practice going bold and it will get easier every time.
- Make a bucket list and start checking it off.
- Hire a coach. They are great at helping you move forward.
- The world does not benefit from you hiding your badassery. Be proud of it and let it shine.
- You only live once; you might as well enjoy the high of being a badass.
- Do it scared and you will delight yourself.

*Badassery is engaging in seemingly impossible activities and achieving success in a manner that renders all onlookers completely awestruck.*
*~ Ronda Rousey*

# Push 13
## Decide. The Rest is Details

The moment you actually decide, everything changes. You stop waffling and get clear. Your power and energy shift and you say, "No matter what, this will happen!"

1. Think of a time you reached a dream or a goal. You can probably still remember the moment you decided.
2. Decision makes fear take a back seat.
3. Deciding gives you super powers because you won't give up.
4. Don't look for others' approval. This is your life, so you get to decide.
5. Ask yourself, "Will this bring me happiness and fulfillment?" If so, the answer is an unequivocal "yes."
6. Deciding brings clarity and clarity is the heart of action.

## More About Deciding

- You already have everything you need inside of you to make the right decision for you. So go bold.
- Once you are firm, you begin to take action and fear slinks back in the corner.
- Choosing between where you are and where you want to be is not an easy decision, but it is a worthwhile one.
- Sometimes you need to claim you and do what's best for yourself, rather than everyone else.
- Decide to walk away from that which no longer serves you.

*Have the courage to follow your heart and intuition. They somehow already know what you truly want to become.*

*~ Steve Jobs*

# Push 14
## Make YES Your Mantra

You can look at life as a list of problems, fears and failures or as experiences, opportunities and adventures. Choose the latter and make "yes" your mantra.

1. Replace your automatic "no" or "I don't know" response with yes.
2. The more you say yes, the more practice you get at going bold and pretty soon, basically nothing scares you anymore.
3. What have you really got to lose? It may feel like a lot right now, but truthfully, it may not really be much, and you have everything to gain. Weigh the scales.
4. The three most important words to say to yourself are: "Yes, I can."

## More About What YES Can Do For You

- Always say yes to the longings of your own heart. Life is short.
- Mantra: I will say yes to all good things coming my way.
- Don't be afraid. If it goes wrong, remember that you'll handle it, and you'll grow.
- You are really the only person you can depend on, so say yes to you every time.
- Say yes to letting go of those people or things in your life that no longer serve you.
- Say yes to being the authentic you. This knocks fear down to its knees.

*Say yes. You'll figure it out afterward.*
*~ Tina Fey*

# Push 15
## You've Totally Got This

You have an inner strength that you may not even know you have. You've survived your life this far, so it's there. Acknowledge your power and rely on it daily.

1.  Fear makes you think you don't want to do it, but you actually do!
2.  Look how much you've already survived. Don't be afraid that you can't make it through this.
3.  You are naturally creative, resourceful and whole. You have everything you need inside of you already to live a brave, meaningful life.
4.  You were given this life because you are strong enough to live it.

## More About How You've Got This

- This is the beginning of anything and everything you want – even if it was thrown at you unexpectedly.
- Inhale confidence, exhale doubt.
- Life is tough, but so are you.
- You've got what it takes and it may take everything you've got.
- It's time to stop pretending you're an average person. You've got a big life ahead.
- Always believe that something wonderful is about to happen.

*You're allowed 5 emotional minutes of the day and then you gotta be gansta.*

*~ A'Gaci*

**You've finished. Before you go…**

Tweet/share that you finished this book.

Please star rate this book.

Reviews are solid gold to writers. Please take a few minutes to give us some itty bitty feedback.

# ABOUT THE AUTHOR

After raising six children and launching them out, life pulled the rug out from under me and shattered my world. I discovered my husband had fallen in love with another woman. I freaked out, hit the floor and curled up in the fetal position for 6 months. During all those years of raising kids, I had kept nothing of myself and never earned a penny. I had no career, and now suddenly I needed one. I felt desperate and cornered, lacking even one ounce of courage.

One night I had an "aha" moment, "Wait, I don't have to stay here because the kids are grown and I can't heal in this town." That led me to put everything I owned in storage, sell my car, shut down my phone and travel in developing countries by myself for a year. While on my global journey, I had to learn to overcome all of my fears and find my own identity.

Upon my return to the States, I became a certified life and leadership coach. I am also an author and an international speaker.

I wrote a memoir of that amazing and crazy solo journey around the world, entitled, "It's Already Tomorrow Here: Never Underestimate the Power of Running Away." It can be found on Amazon and Audible.

If you liked this Itty Bitty® book you might also enjoy…

- **Your Amazing Itty Bitty® Self-Esteem Book** – Jade Elizabeth

- **Your Amazing Itty Bitty® Self-Hypnosis Book** – Amy Mayne Robinson

- **Your Amazing Itty Bitty® Affirmations Book** – Micaela Passeri

And dozens of other Itty Bitty® Books available online.

Made in the USA
Middletown, DE
30 September 2017